D1134430

TRICKS
and MAGIC

by JAMES WEBSTER
with illustrations by ROBERT AYTON

Publishers: Wills & Hepworth Ltd., Loughborough

First published 1969 *Printed in England*

A magic wand and a magician's hat

Every magician uses a magic wand from time to time, waving it when saying magic words. You can make one by wrapping some white drawing paper four or five times round a knitting needle and then gluing down the edge or sticking it down with gummed tape. Pull out the knitting needle, trim the ends of the wand, and then paint it in attractive colours.

You can also make a magician's hat like the one in the illustration. Take a large sheet of newspaper (wrapping or drawing paper would be better), about 24 ins. by 12 ins. (approximately 60 cms. by 30 cms.), and fold it up as shown in the diagram below. Draw the curved, dotted line B—C, as shown. A good way to draw this line is to put a pin through a piece of string at A, and a pencil point through the string at B. You can then easily draw the correct curved line to C.

Cut along the line B—C and open up the section. You can now fold your hat, making the pointed part at A. Adjust the amount of overlap so that the hat fits your head, and then glue down the overlapping section.

Star and moon shapes can be cut from coloured paper and stuck on the hat, or you can paint the shapes onto it.

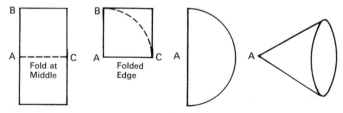

If you hold the end of the wand *very loosely* and wave it slowly up and down, it will appear to bend like the one in the top picture.

Think of a number...

Ask a friend to think of a number between 1 and 99, *but not to tell you*. Tell him you can find out the number he is thinking of, if he will do a sum for you.

Give him a pencil and paper, and tell him to write down his age. In the illustration opposite is an example of how this trick is done, and we have imagined that a boy's age is 11.

After your friend has written down his own age, you tell him to double it and write down the answer. To that figure he must then add 5, and then multiply the total by 100. A quick way to multiply by 100 is just to add on two noughts.

You then ask him to divide his total by 2, and from the total he must then take away the number of days in the year. To the resulting total he then adds the number he first thought of. In our example we have imagined this was 90, but it can be any number between 1 and 99.

Your friend must then tell you his total, and *you* add 115.

The two figures on the left of *your* total give his age (one figure if he is under ten) and the two figures on the right of your total give the number he first thought of!

In this example, we will imagine you have a friend aged 11, who thought of the number 90.

AGE -------	11
DOUBLE IT ------	22
ADD 5 ------	27
MULTIPLY BY 100 ---	2700
DIVIDE BY 2 ----	1350
DEDUCT NUMBER OF DAYS IN YEAR (365) ---	985
ADD THE NUMBER FIRST THOUGHT OF (90) ----	1075

Your friend tells you his total and you add 115.
(Example : 1075 + 115 = 1190)
The two figures on the left of YOUR total (1190) give his age (11) and the two figures on the right give the number he first thought of (90).

Climbing through a postcard

Hold up a postcard and say to your audience, "I will cut a hole in this postcard and climb through it." At this, they will either look at you with wonder or laugh their heads off, and either way they will not believe you—but it can be done.

All you need is a postcard, a penknife and scissors and a cutting surface—a thick piece of card will do for this.

Fig. 1.   Cut a line lengthwise down the centre with your penknife, but do not go over either edge.

Fig. 2.   Fold the card over along the cut, and cut a number of lines, as shown, through the double thickness. Scissors could be used. Again stop each cut before the edge.

Fig. 3.   Turn the card round, and cut between each of the cuts you have made. Stop before coming to the folded edge.

Fig. 4.   Carefully open up the card, and very, very carefully pull out the ends, as shown. If some cut lines have not gone right through, then cut again.

Fig. 5.   The card will stretch out a surprisingly long way, and then you can slowly, carefully step into it and wriggle it up over your body and head. You will have climbed through a post-card!
          Then you can lay it on the table and fold it back to its original shape.

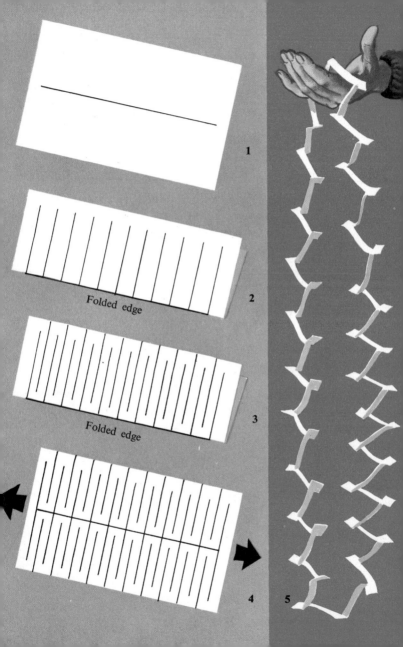

1

2

Folded edge

3

Folded edge

4

5

The magic symbol

Cut out nine small squares and number them 1 to 9, as shown. Then ask your friends to arrange them so that each line across, each line down and both diagonal lines —add up to 15.

It can be done, but it takes ages and ages unless you have the magic symbol. You produce the symbol and say that by concentrating on it you will be able to solve the problem; then with knotted brows you proceed to place each numbered square down until all nine are in place.

You simply follow the symbol's design in a series of straight lines, starting at its tail at the top with 1, then down the line to 2, then up and across to 3, down to 4, then up and across to the centre, stopping in the middle for 5, and straight on for 6, and so on till 9. (See diagram.) The problem is solved, each of the rows adds up to the required 15, thanks to the magic symbol.

To draw the symbol, mark nine dots as shown, then join as indicated, colour and cut out.

Rearrange these numbers so that they total 15, horizontally, vertically and diagonally.

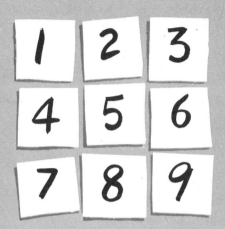

The magic symbol

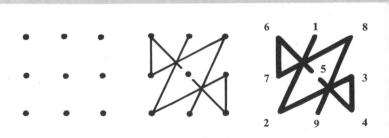

Mind reading

'Mind Reading' is a good trick to do at a party. You need a friend to help you.

Your friend blindfolds you, and then hides a penny in some part of the room. Someone else can do this if they wish, provided your friend knows the hiding place.

Now your friend walks round the room calling out to you, "Is it here? Under this? Is this where it is? Here? What about here?"

"Yes!" you say, at just the right time and to everyone's astonishment. You know when to say "Yes" because your partner will begin his question with "What" when he is pointing to the place where the penny is hidden.

Now ask for the penny to be hidden again without you seeing the hiding place. This time you are not blindfolded, and your partner does not say anything. He merely points to different places and touches different things. Suddenly you say "That's the place!" Your partner has signalled this to you by some pre-viously arranged sign—such as looking at his feet or perhaps blinking rapidly three times—before indicating the hiding place.

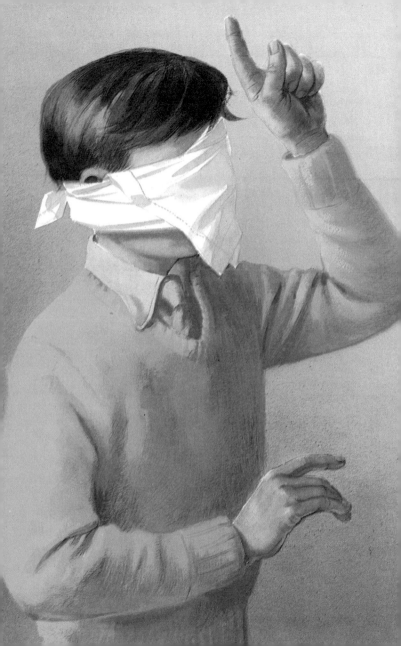

The disappearing pencil

Pick up a pencil and wave it about before your audience, saying you are about to make it disappear for ever. They will not believe you, so you then proceed to prove it.

Lay half a sheet of newspaper on the table, and roll up the pencil tightly from corner to corner, pinching or twisting the ends so that it does not fall out.

Now for the great moment. Hold up the roll of paper, and commence to tear off short lengths, inch by inch, until there is none left.

The pencil has gone!—and your audience is absolutely amazed.

The secret is this. You have already made an imitation pencil, and have simply torn through it and the sheet of newspaper at the same time.

The imitation pencil is quite simple to make. All that is needed is a piece of paper about 6 ins. by 3 ins., (approximately 15 cms. by 7.5 cms.), a very small stump of pencil which is sharpened, a tube of glue and some coloured ink.

Using a long, round pencil, roll it very tightly in the paper and stick in the short, sharpened pencil stump (Fig. 1 and 2). Stick down the edge with gum or paste (Fig. 3). When dry, paint it (red is best—Fig. 4), and draw out the long pencil when the ink is dry. You now have a long imitation pencil made of paper, and it looks just like the real thing, but only you know this!

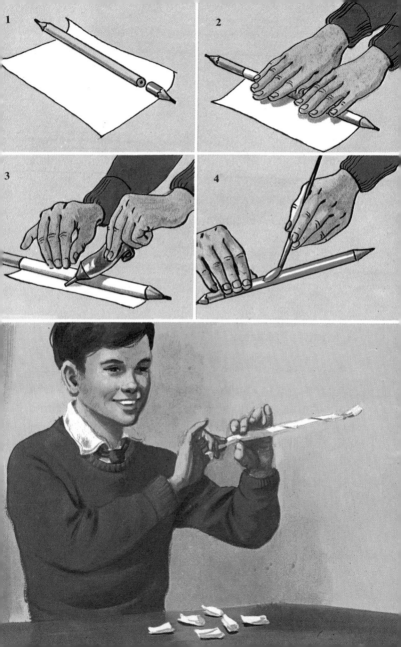

'Singing' glasses

Ask a friend if he thinks a glass can sing. He will, of course, say "No!"

Put a little water in the bottom of a glass. Wet your finger and rub it gently round the top of the rim, holding the glass steady with your other hand. Vary the speed of the circle you make and the pressure of your finger until the glass begins to 'sing' with a varying, loud note.

A thin glass sings best, but it is easily broken, so be careful how you handle it.

A knot-tying trick

Lay a scarf or large handkerchief on the table, and ask a friend if he can take hold of the two ends and tie a a knot in the middle without his hands releasing either end. Unless he knows the trick, he will try all sorts of contortions.

When he gives up, you can show him how it is done. Fold the handkerchief or scarf lengthwise and place on the table. Fold your arms as in Fig. 1, pick up an end with each hand, then unfold your arms without releasing the ends. You will find that you have tied a knot in the middle.

FIG. 1

FIG. 2

Reflex tester

This will test your reflexes, and enable you to find out how quickly a message travels from your brain to your fingers. You can also test the speed of your friends' reflexes.

You will need a piece of thick paper about 5 ins. by 3 ins. (approximately 12.5 cms. by 7.5 cms.). Hold it as shown in the illustration and ask your friend to place his hand, as shown, with forefinger and thumb extended over the two sides of the piece of paper. Then tell him to catch the paper as you drop it and, without warning, release the paper. Unless he knows the trick he will probably not be able to catch it.

When your turn comes, if you wish to play a trick on your friend, all you do is drop your hand a few inches when he lets go, and at the same time snap your finger and thumb together. With practice you will catch it every time.

However, if you seriously want to test your reflexes, then there must be no trickery. Instead of using a piece of paper, cut a piece of card 12 ins. by 2 ins. (approximately 30 cms. by 5 cms.), and mark it as shown. You could even use a ruler which, owing to its weight, will drop more quickly than the card. You should be able to catch the ruler without having to drop your hand at the same time. Make a note of the number where you catch it, and make about six attempts each. Total up your scores, the highest being the winner.

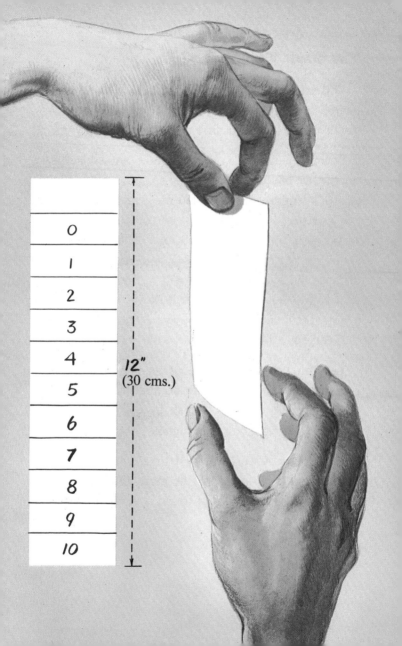

0
1
2
3
4
12"
(30 cms.)
5
6
7
8
9
10

The magic blind spot

This trick is really an optical illusion and very few people know of it. When you try it out on your friends, it will amaze them, but first you must try it on yourself.

From a pack of playing cards take out a black two, say the two of clubs or the two of spades. Hold it side-up at arm's length, close your left eye and with your open eye look very hard at the spot on the left; now move it very slowly towards you, still looking hard at the left spot. For a while you will see both, but at a certain distance the spot on the right will vanish then re-appear as it comes closer. Now move it slowly away from you again; it will vanish and re-appear. The explanation is that there is a blind spot in everyone's vision.

Try this on your friend, pretending that you are responsible. Tell him what to do and that as he does it you will make the spot vanish by concentrating very hard and thinking magic thoughts.

If it does not work the first time, you can say that making things disappear is the most difficult magic of all, but make sure that your friend is doing it properly.

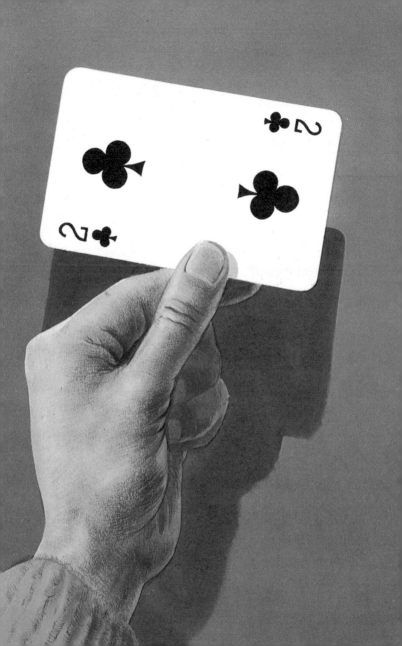

A magic circle

Set out six counters in two rows, as shown in 'A'. Round coins will do just as well.

Now invite a friend to make the coins or counters into a circle (as Fig. B). He is allowed three moves, but each time he moves a coin or counter it must be placed so that it touches two others.

The correct moves are shown in Fig. 1, 2, 3 and 4, but, funnily enough, even when you show your friend what to do, he will be unable to make the circle without a lot of practice.

Try it yourself without looking at the picture.

The balancing card

Here is a really simple trick with a playing card.

Challenge a friend to balance a card on its edge. He may try as long as he pleases, but he will not succeed.

Whilst he is busy doing this, pick up a card yourself, and hold it in the palm of your hand, pressing the ends so that it bends slightly. Then stand the card on the curved edge.

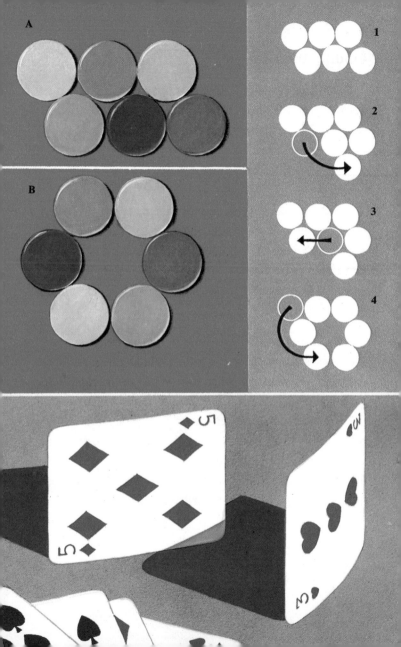

Finding the card

Deal three cards in a row, face upwards, and continue doing this (as in the illustration) until you have used 21 cards and have three small packs of 7 cards each.

As you deal, ask a friend to remember one particular card. Then ask him which of the three packs it is in.

Place this pack face downwards between the other two, also face downwards, and deal the same 21 cards again. Ask your friend which pack his card is in now. Place this pack between the other two and deal once more. Again your friend indicates the pack which contains his card.

Repeat this process twice more, that is, deal the cards four times altogether, each time placing the pack he indicates between the other two. When your friend tells you where his card is for the fourth time, again place this pack in the middle between the other packs, and then turn up the cards one by one. The eleventh card will be the one your friend chose. You can make this trick more impressive if you avoid counting aloud and appear to think hard about each card you turn up.

The one-two-three trick

In the picture you can see a hand holding what looks like the Ace, two and three of Diamonds. Actually the Ace is the Ace of Hearts, the other two cards having been carefully arranged over it. You can use this arrangement to play an impressive card trick.

Place the real Ace of Diamonds at the bottom of the pack (face downwards). Then, without your audience seeing, arrange the Ace of Hearts and the two and three of Diamonds as shown, displaying these three cards to your audience and letting them think the cards are the Ace, two and three of Diamonds. Then fold the three cards together (face downwards), and let your audience see you place the top one anywhere in the middle of the rest of the pack, the second card at the bottom of the pack, and the third one at the top—all face downwards.

Now tell your audience you will bring the Ace, two and three of Diamonds together. Invite someone to cut the pack anywhere, placing the bottom half of the pack on the top of the other half. Then turn the pack and deal out the cards, face upwards, and somewhere in it will be the Ace, two, three of Diamonds all together!

The lower picture
shows how the three
cards will appear somewhere
in the middle of the pack.

Cards that know their names

Arrange a pack of thirteen cards in this order: 3, 8, 7, Ace, Queen, 6, 4, 2, Jack, King, 10, 9, 5.

Now hold the pack face downwards, so that the bottom card is the 5.

You can now tell your audience that each of these cards will answer its name. Begin by spelling out "A-C-E", taking one card from the top of the pack for each of the three A-C-E letters and putting it at the bottom. The next card, as your audience will see when you turn it over, will be the Ace. Putting that card on the table, *face upwards*, leave it there and then continue by spelling out "T-W-O" in the same way as before. the fourth card will be a 2, and after you have shown it to your audience, you must put it on the table, face upwards. Continue then spelling out "T-H-R-E-E", this time putting five cards at the bottom of the pack— one for each letter—and showing your audience the sixth, which will be a 3.

You can continue with the same procedure through 4, 5, 6, 7, 8, 9, 10, Jack, Queen, and King, putting a card from the top to the bottom of the pack for each letter you are spelling out. In each case the appropriate card showing the number or picture you want, will appear at the right time—even when you have only two cards left to count with.

The unbroken, broken matchstick!

This trick is simple to perform, and all you need is a matchstick and a clean handkerchief with a hem.

To prepare, you secretly hide a matchstick inside the hem of a handkerchief, sliding it in from one corner for about an inch or so. Then, holding the hem between thumb and forefinger of each hand (but making sure that the finger and thumb of your right hand is holding the hem at the place where the match is concealed) wave the handkerchief in front of your audience, telling them to observe that it is quite empty.

Place the handkerchief open on the table (though still holding the hem) and ask someone to place their own match in the middle. When they have done this, with your left hand fold three corners into the middle and over the matchstick, and then with your right hand fold in the fourth corner containing the match in the hem. Fold the whole handkerchief over again, but making sure you can still feel the match in the hem. With the handkerchief folded tightly round it, offer this match to the same member of your audience, telling him to break it and make sure it really is in two halves. He will, of course, think he is breaking the matchstick *he* placed in the middle.

Now tell your audience you can mend the broken match. Wave your hand over the handkerchief, place it on the table and slowly open it out flat. There, in the middle—and to the great surprise of your audience—will be an unbroken matchstick!

In case you are challenged to do the trick again—it is wise to have another match already concealed in another part of the hem.

Matchstick handcuffs

This trick needs to be practised, but you should soon be able to do it with your eyes closed.

The object is to take each matchstick from the other hand with thumb and forefinger without becoming trapped as in Fig. 4, and then to replace quickly.

Study Fig. 2, which shows your hands as they will appear if you practise in front of a mirror. Notice how the thumb of one hand reaches through the opening for the match end, and the forefinger of the same hand reaches round the outside of the other thumb.

Another way to master the trick is to do it in reverse; start as in Fig. 3 and try to fit the matches back as in Fig. 2.

When you have mastered the trick, perform it in front of a friend, then ask him to do it. It looks easy and he will say so, but he will trap himself every time!

USE SAFETY MATCHES ONLY

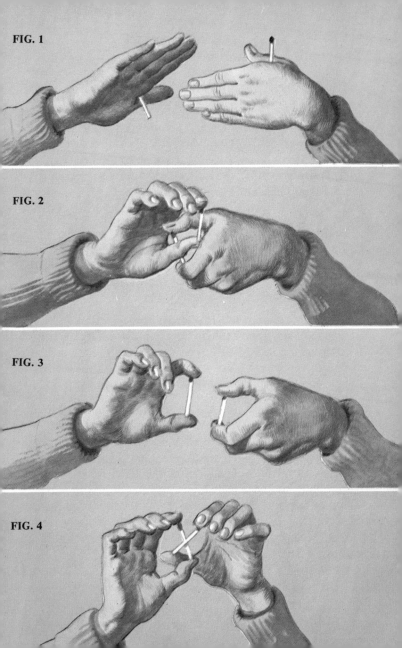

FIG. 1

FIG. 2

FIG. 3

FIG. 4

The vanishing handkerchief

You will need three identical match-boxes and two small, identical handkerchiefs for this trick.

To prepare for the trick (and without your friends seeing), place one full box in your pocket. Empty the second match-box and wedge a row of matches evenly and carefully against the *back* of the tray—as shown in the picture. Then put a small handkerchief in the empty tray. Leave the third box empty on the table.

Begin by showing the *back* of the trick box to your audience. "Here is a full box of matches," you say. Shut the box with your thumb, taking care to press all the matches in at the same time, and place the box on the table.

Let your audience see you fold a second handkerchief and place it in the empty match-box. See that the tray is inserted the same way up as the tray in the trick box already prepared. "Here is a box with a handkerchief in it," you say, and then place the box in your pocket.

Wave your wand and say some magic words. "Now the handkerchief has changed places with the matches," you announce. Open the box on the table and pull out the other handkerchief, taking care not to let them see the matches you wedged down the back of the tray. When your audience asks to see the match-box in which they saw you put the handkerchief, you can puzzle them even further by producing from your pocket the full box of matches which you put there previously—*not* the one with the handkerchief in it.

USE SAFETY MATCHES ONLY

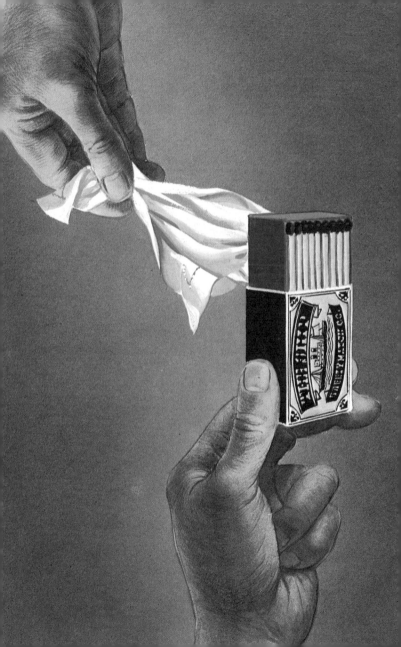

A balancing trick

This is a simple trick that needs little practice, yet when performed it will amaze your friends.

Place a match-box on the back of your hand (as shown in the top illustration), and tell your friends you can make it stand on end without touching it. Let them try to do it first. After many attempts they will give up and say it is impossible.

Then you amaze them by raising your hand with the match-box in position, saying, "Hey presto," clenching your fist and showing them the match-box standing on its end.

This is how it is done: while your friends were trying to balance the box on end, you were secretly preparing.

Open an *empty* match-box about a quarter of an inch, lay the open end down on the back of your hand just over the loose flesh on your knuckles, and close the match-box so that it squeezes a little of your flesh into the box. Fully closed it should look as if it is just resting there. Then close your fist—the box will magically stand on end, as in the illustration opposite.

Practise a few times and do not forget to pretend that this trick is very, very difficult.

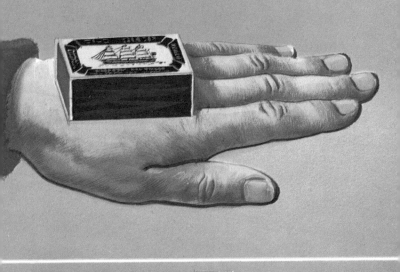

A puzzling match-box

A minute or two with a sharp knife and a match-box and you will have a trick that will puzzle everyone.

Empty the match-box and remove the tray. Cut this carefully in half. Turn one half upside-down, inserting the matches as shown in the illustration, and then replace the trays inside the box. To keep the two half trays firmly together, it is a good idea to join the sides of each with a small piece of gummed tape.

Open the box about half an inch and place it on the table. "This box is the right way up, isn't it?" you say.

Shut the box and open it once more to remind your audience which way up it is. Shut it again, and slowly turn it over, endways. Turn it over again, and for a third time.

"Now, which way up is it now?" you ask.

"Upside down," anyone watching carefully will say.

Push open the tray a little to show that the box is still apparently the right way up, shake your head and try them again. When they still get it wrong, turn the box over once only. They will be completely confused to find that the box is *still* apparently the right way up.

USE SAFETY MATCHES ONLY

CUT MATCHBOX TRAY IN HALF

INVERT ONE HALF AS SHEWN
REPLACE MATCHES AND CLOSE BOX

The vanishing matches

Prepare for this trick by pushing a half-full match-box up your sleeve. You may need a broad elastic band round your arm to keep the box securely in position.

Now take an empty match-box and shake it. The matches up your sleeve will rattle loudly. "Guess how many matches are in this box," you say.

When your friends have made their guesses, you can give them the box to see who is right. They will look very surprised to find it is empty!

You can vary this trick by placing a full and an empty match-box on the table. You make the empty one appear to rattle when you shake it. Then pick up the full one *with your other hand*, say some magic words over it and shake it. Being quite full it will not rattle— though your audience will not realise this and will wonder how you have seemingly made the match-boxes change places.

USE SAFETY MATCHES ONLY

The magic purse

Ask a friend to lend you a small coin, fold it carefully in a square of paper, wave it in the air saying some magic words, then place it on the table and unfold—the coin has vanished! Tell the owner of the coin not to worry. Fold up the paper, wave it about with more magic words—open up and 'Hey presto!' the coin is back.

This is a mystifying trick but it needs to be carefully prepared and practised beforehand.

You will need a sheet of notepaper about 8 inches by 4 inches (approximately 20 cms. by 10 cms.). Fold it exactly in half, then with a needle prick through both thicknesses, four little holes each 2 inches (5 cms.) apart so as to form a square. Then cut the paper along the fold, making two pieces the same size. Fold in the edges of one piece, using the needle pricks as guides, and running your fingernail firmly along the folds to make them flat. Folded four times like this it will make a sort of square paper purse. Now stick this with paste or gum on to the unfolded sheet, exactly between the needle holes, as Fig. 2, and press down hard until dry.

You are now ready. Hiding the folded purse underneath, place the borrowed coin onto the plain side, as Fig. 1. Fold over the edges, making another purse with the coin inside. Your audience will not know of the hidden purse. Pick up and wave about, saying some magic words; place down on the table empty side upwards, and unfold. This is where you tell the owner of the coin not to worry. Refold and repeat the waving and magic words, then open up the purse containing the coin.

42

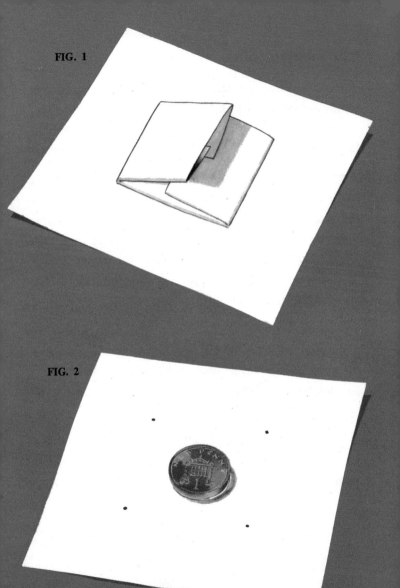

FIG. 1

FIG. 2

The melting coin

Hold a penny between the finger and thumb of one hand, as shown or with finger and thumb on the edges of the coin. The curved backs of your fingers should be towards your audience.

Move your other hand towards the coin with fingers and thumb extended, as if about to grasp the coin. At the last moment relax your grip so that the coin falls into the palm of your hand, exactly at the time that your other fingers and thumb close on nothing. Sweep this hand into the air as if throwing the coin away, and it appears to melt into nothing.

Now say a magic word, (abracadabra is a good one), and reach out into the air with the hand that contains the coin, letting it slide down to your finger and thumb, so that you can appear to pick the coin out of the air again!

After a little practice, when you can quickly and smoothly, do this trick, you will really be able to mystify your friends.

The coin that does not move

Have you ever seen an entertainer, on the stage or television, take hold of a tablecloth and with a lightning sweep of his arm pull away the cloth, leaving an array of crockery standing on the table exactly where it was before he pulled away the cloth? If you have not seen this feat, then rest assured that it can be done, but for goodness sake do not try it—it takes a lot of practice and a lot of broken crocks before it can be perfected!

Instead, with a small coin and a playing card you can do a similar experiment which is more simple, less costly and still as fascinating.

Place the coin in the centre of the playing card, then balance the card and coin on your finger, as shown in the picture. Make sure that the coin is immediately over your finger. Then, when you are ready, strike the edge of the card with a finger of your other hand. The card will spin away across the room, and surprise! surprise! the coin rests quietly on the end of your finger.

You can do this trick with a coin on the lip of a bottle, or even on the end of a pencil.

The popular variation of this trick is to drop a coin into a jam jar without touching it.

All it needs is a little practice.

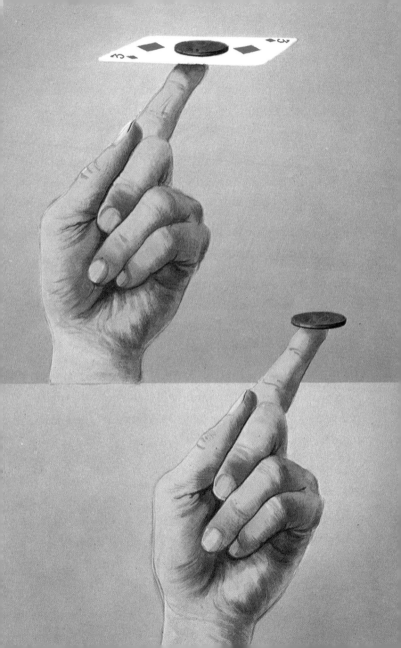

Wet coin — dry coin !

Put a dinner plate on the table and place a coin in it —slightly to one side. Then pour in just enough water to cover the coin (Fig. 1).

Say to your audience that you can pick the coin from the plate with your fingers without getting them wet!

They will not believe you, but will have doubts when you produce from beneath the table a jam jar, a slice of cork and a box of matches.

First stick two matches into the cork (you may have to sharpen them), then float it on the water and set light to the matches (Fig. 2). When the matches are burning steadily, invert the jam jar and lower it down over them.

After a second or two the matches will go out, and to everyone's surprise the water will have left the plate and gone into the jam jar (Fig. 3). The coin is left high and dry, waiting for you to pick it up.

This trick should be practised before trying it out in front of your friends.

Because you need lighted matches to do this trick, *only do it when an adult is present*. The scientific principle behind this trick is explained in the Ladybird book— 'Air, Wind and Flight'.

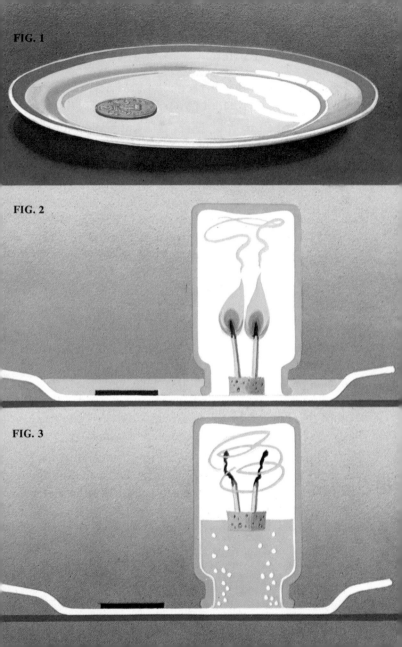

FIG. 1

FIG. 2

FIG. 3

Blowing over a brick

For this trick you will need a house brick. There is probably one somewhere in your garden.

Produce it before your friends, saying, "You all see this brick; it's very, very heavy, yet I can stand it up and blow it over!" Invite them to try. They will soon give up!

When your turn comes, stand the brick on end, about 6 ins. (or about 15 cms.) from the edge of an old table or box, tilt it and slide the end of a bag under it. Then blow up the paper bag—and over will go the brick!

Picking up a bottle with a straw

Walk into the room with a bottle in one hand and a drinking straw in the other, and say to your friends that you can pick the bottle off the table with the flimsy straw and without touching it with your hands. They will all think it impossible, particularly after they have tried! You can then show them how to do it.

Carefully bend back about a third of the straw, insert the bend of the straw into the neck of the bottle, as shown in the illustration, push down the straw until the end springs into the shoulder of the bottle, then gently lift—and up comes the bottle.

Practise this trick before doing it in front of friends, and use a medicine bottle with a shoulder as shown in the illustration.

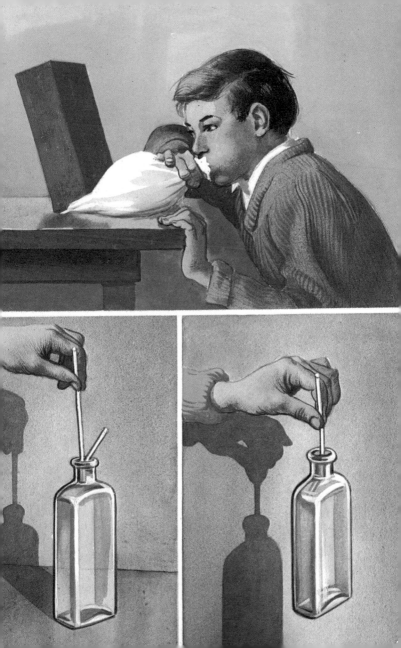

BRODARD ET TAUPIN — IMPRIMEUR - RELIEUR
Paris-Coulommiers. — Imprimé en France.
6739-1-2 - Dépôt légal n° 6289, 1er trimestre 1967.
Le Livre de Poche - 4, rue de Galliéra, Paris.
30 - 11 - 0183 - 13

TABLE DES MATIÈRES